Airbnb Toolbox

HOW TO FUEL YOUR AIRBNB LISTING TO WORK FOR YOU

A WORKBOOK FOR HOSTS

D1714360

SANDRA SHILLINGTON

CONTENTS

Introduction

My Story and Why You Need This Workbook

I'm part of that subculture of people who "share" a home on Airbnb. Since 2013, I've generated some serious income hosting on Airbnb. Last year I generated over $50,000 in revenue with one listing. I have a job, a family and other responsibilities - and I manage my Airbnb rental at the same time - which is what lead me to create the Airbnb Toolbox™ and the Perfect Host Process™. It came out of necessity. I was wearing a lot of hats. I was switching from one task to another all day long. Did you know that research has shown that multitasking ends up making us less productive by fragmenting our attention? I learned this the hard way. That's why I knew I needed to find ways to accomplish more in less time. So I found some ways that allowed me to actually do less, and accomplish more.

My objective is to have every guest feel like I have exceeded their expectations, compelling them to give me positive reviews and tell all their friends about my terrific vacation rental. That's why I created a system that generates predictable and positive results.

If you're new to Airbnb or have been too busy to think you could take your hosting to the next level, the Airbnb Toolbox™ will set you up for success. Whatever your goals are - whether it's saving for college, paying yourself more money, or freeing up your schedule for other passions, this workbook will give you the tools you need to put the power of Airbnb to work for you. Through my experience and research I've compiled the best of everything I learned into the Perfect Host Process™ to save you hours of costly trial and error learning.

Airbnb & The Sharing Economy

As you may already know, Airbnb was founded in 2008 and has over 2 million listings worldwide. Through its trusted community of travelers and hosts, earning an income through short term home renting is accessible to more people than ever before.

You've probably also heard of its competitor HomeAway (Expedia) - founded in 2005, estimated to have over 1 million listings. There's also FlipKey (TripAdvisor) and several others, yet many have merged with the larger companies. HomeAway (Expedia) began with a more traditional vacation rental approach, where owners paid to advertise on their site - listing second homes strictly used for vacation rentals, while hosts on Airbnb rented single rooms and their primary residence for a per stay fee. Airbnb paved the way for this new "sharing economy", and with that, the industry is ever changing. In fact, HomeAway (Expedia) is now shifting to a community based model somewhat similar to Airbnb.

Airbnb Travelers Are Often:

- Looking for a unique place to stay.
- Looking for an affordable, local experience that can't be duplicated.
- Wanting to feel less like a visitor and more like a local.
- In search of an authentic getaway and experience.

A Word About Local Laws...

You may know that the surge in popularity of home sharing has not been without controversy. In many cities the laws on short term renting are being re-evaluated. That's why you should always stay informed on the laws in your local area. Fortunately, Airbnb has been involved in this process and helps keep hosts informed on this topic and others related to home sharing. In some cities, Airbnb is now collecting occupancy taxes from travelers and remitting them to the appropriate tax authority. Governments differ on the tax rate, how often it's paid and forms required. For more information, visit the website of your city and county and look up "occupancy tax", "hotel tax", or "transient lodging tax." Also, stay informed through AirbnbCitizen.com.

For more information on responsible hosting in the United States, visit https://www.airbnb.com/help/article/1376/responsible-hosting-in-the-united-states. You are responsible for understanding your local laws and complying with them.

The Perfect Host Process™

The Perfect Host Process™ leads to predictable, positive results for your Airbnb business. It's based on these three actions. This workbook will lead you through the process of developing these best practices.

Action 1 - Build Your Foundation

1. Write an Engaging Personal Profile
    Worksheet #1

2. Write a Stellar Listing Title
    Worksheet #2

3. Write an Inspiring Listing Description
    Worksheet #3

4. Persuasive Listing Photos

5. Accurate Descriptions

6. Establish House Rules
    House Rules Cheat Sheet

7. Maximize Your Profit
    Worksheet #4

8. Optimize Your Listing
    Airbnb SEO Checklist

Action 2 - Enhance The Guest Experience

Action 3 - Assemble Your Tools

Bonus Material: The Library of Templates

Includes copy and paste templates for:

How To Use This Workbook

You'll Build Your Foundation, using our interactive worksheets to build the perfect listing and profile. You'll Enhance the Guest Experience by looking at every touch point you have with your guests - from answering inquiries, sending emails, to responding to guest questions. This will lead to conversations that pay off, and ultimately, predictable positive reviews.

You'll Assemble Your Tools by putting our tools to work for you using our Library of Templates and a Guest Welcome Book. Finally, you'll Evaluate Your System, making sure everything is working for you.

Throughout this workbook, you'll see **Worksheets, Checklists** and **Cheat Sheets,** that will help you complete everything at your own pace. They are in a fillable format where you can complete them directly on the worksheet. The questions will help direct your thought process and get your ideas and plan on paper. When you reach the end of the workbook, your completed Worksheets, Checklists and Cheat Sheets will become the finished product and working documents for you to put the **Perfect Host Process**™ into place. In the **Library of Templates Bonus Material** you'll find a complete set of messaging templates to cut, paste and customize them to your needs. You'll also find a complete template you can customize to create your **House Rules** and **Guest Welcome Book**. This "done for you content" will save you hours of preparation time! You can access the templates at https://airbnbtemplates.writerrs.com.

Are you ready? Let's get started!

Action 1: Build Your Foundation

Let The Competition Begin

D id you know there are over 2.3 million properties listed on Airbnb? The popularity of Airbnb has created a lot of competition. When travelers enter a search they can view pages and pages of properties. High quality pictures are - without a doubt - what grabs their attention and showcase your property. The photos on most listings are so good, that you cannot underestimate the importance of professional quality photos. After the photos, it's up to your description to tell and sell. If you don't succeed at getting your property in their mind's eye, they'll move on to the next property. That's why your listing must be organized and well written, so that travelers can easily read the information they're looking for. You want to capture their attention so they don't move on to the next listing. I'm going to show you exactly how to do that here. By the end of this section, you'll have an organized, well written listing description that will compel travelers to want to learn more about it.

Let The Conversation Begin

Once a traveler lands on your listing page, the conversation begins. Think of your listing description as the beginning of a conversation, rather than a transaction. Conversation is the key to building genuine trust and making true connections. Rather than writing to a mass audience, imagine that you're sitting across a table telling a friend about your home. Use a friendly, personal tone that tells a story. You're painting an inviting picture that will show travelers the experience they will have in your home. But remember to keep it real. You don't want to be misleading in any way. Overselling leads to unhappy guests and negative reviews. Instead, describe some of your favorite parts of your home and why. Talk about what other people have said they enjoyed while staying there.

"Disappointment equals expectation minus reality."
Chip Conley,
Airbnb's Head of Global Hospitality & Strategy

Write An Engaging Personal Profile

Although Airbnb has become more widely accepted, there's always some uncertainty when dealing with people you don't know. A good host profile breaks down barriers and provides a comfort level with both you and the traveler.

Your Profile Photo

Make sure your profile photo is well lit, clearly shows your face and offers a welcoming smile. You want to appear friendly and approachable.

Your Description

This is your first impression to the traveler. What would you say if you were introducing yourself in person? Help travelers get to know a little about you and why you love your neighborhood. Describe some of your interests and why you like to host or travel. Add some fun facts about yourself. It can help guests feel they know you better if they know a bit about your work or where you went to school. What do you like to do in your spare time? What makes you a good host? Where are you from?

Get Verified

Be sure to use the Verified ID feature on Airbnb. Provide as many identity verifications as possible, such as email address, social media, and valid physical identification. This improves your trustworthiness to the online community.

Here are some example profile descriptions:

"I'm a cosmetics industry executive turned full-time rancher. I love animals and love being on my ranch, hosting guests that will enjoy privacy, open space and outdoor fun."

"I'm a life-long Southern Californian and Los Angeles beach lover. I enjoy visits to Venice Beach, going to the local restaurants, and bike riding on the boardwalk. I take pride in my property and always respond to guests needs. I live in the building, so I interact with guests directly – from key exchanges, to cleaning, to questions, and anything in between."

"Native Californian, tech geek, surfer and outdoorsman. I love great food and cocktails. I know where to send people for a real local's experience. I love sharing travel destinations and adventures."

Now It's Your Turn….

Write Your Engaging Personal Profile

Worksheet #1

On the following page, I've provided cues to help you easily write an impactful personal profile. Answer the questions, and then transfer your final version to your listings. This is a fillable form, so you can enter your answers directly on the worksheet.

Perfect Host Process™ - Worksheet #1

Write Your Engaging Personal Profile

Instructions: Complete the 3 steps below to write your own personal profile. Simply answer the questions, and then transfer your final version to your listings. This is a fillable form, so you can enter your answers directly below the questions.

Step 1: Give yourself a descriptive label:

I'm a....

(Native Texan, Accountant, Surf bum, Wine Enthusiast)

_____

_____

Step 2: What do you like to do in your free time?

who likes to...

(cook, hike, work in my garden)

_____

_____

Step 3: How does this relate to your hosting? Why you like to host? This makes me a great host because...

(I know the best hiking trails in town; I love sharing what the Seattle area has to offer)

_____

_____

_____

_____

Write A Stellar Listing Title

This is your property's first impression to the world. It has one goal. To make people click on it to learn more about it. What will make your property stand out from all the others? After the awesome photos, it needs to say enough to make them interested. From there, the rest of your listing will do the work.

So when deciding on your listing title, think about what people would especially like about it. It's not enough to say, "2 Bedroom, 2 Bathroom Cottage." You need to be more specific and descriptive. You have 50 characters to make an impact. But keep in mind, they may only see the first 20 characters of your title when browsing the results. Many people make the mistake of wasting valuable space by including the city name. Travelers already know the city they entered in their search - so don't include the name of the city in your title. But, DO use a related location fact that would create appeal. Is it located near any major destinations or landmarks? Are there any special benefits of your location? What do most people want when they travel to your area?

For example:
"Modern + Cozy Suite Near Downtown/Stadiums"
"Stylish One Bedroom, One Block from Space Needle"
"Relaxing Laguna Studio! Ocean Front!"
"Comfortable Loft in the Gaslamp with Parking"
"Family Friendly Avalon Penthouse"
"Sunny Studio Apartment in the Heart of Capitol Hill"
"Swanky Downtown Studio 14th & U"
"Renovated 1917 Craftsman Bungalow, Near Farmer's Market"

Now It's Your Turn….

Write Your Stellar Listing Title

Worksheet #2

On the following page, I've provided cues to help you easily write an attention getting listing title. Simply answer the questions, and then transfer your final version to your listings. You'll find an electronic version of this form in the Library of Templates at https://airbnbtemplates.writerrs.com.

Perfect Host Process™ - Worksheet #2

Write Your Stellar Listing Title

Instructions: Complete the steps below to write your own listing title. Simply answer the questions, and then transfer your final version to your listings. This is a fillable form, so you can enter your answers directly below the questions. Note: Make the most of the first 20 characters, as that might be all the guest sees on a search result!!

Step 1: Decide on a one word adjective that describes your home: *(i.e. modern, stylish, family-friendly, sunny)*

_____

Step 2: What type of home is it?
(i.e. one bedroom apartment, studio, 3 bedroom house)

_____

_____

Step 3: What is it's special appeal or benefit?
(i.e. near Stadiums, ocean front, view of the pier)

_____

_____

_____

_____

_____

_____

Write An Inspiring Listing Description

Through your description, transport travelers to what their vacation would feel like. Have empathy for travelers and walk in their shoes. Describe the experience they will have at your home, rather than simply listing the features. Organize your description room by room. Take them on an imaginary tour. Use bullet points whenever possible to make it easy for travelers to scan your page and pick out information.

Be very precise when describing the unique appeal of your property. Focus on what makes your place different from others - just as you did when crafting your listing title. Is it convenient to a major destination? What are the unique advantages of staying at your home? For example, do you offer free parking in an area where parking is a challenge? Do you have bikes that your guests can use? Do you have an outdoor hammock in a relaxing spot? Even if your space is simple and modest, you can create a unique one-of-a-kind experience that attracts guests and welcomes them to your neighborhood. You can offer home baked scones and local coffee, or local craft brews representing your town. Some hosts provide soft, spa-like robes for guests to relax in. If you already have some reviews, notice what past guests liked about your home. Use their comments in your description. Be creative to stand out from the crowd!

Take a look at a description below. It gives you the facts, but it's very basic and offers little personality. There is nothing about it that helps you envision what staying there would feel like.

"This is a one bedroom apartment with a view of the city. There is a living room, a fully equipped kitchen with dishwasher, and a dining table that seats 8 people. The master bedroom has a king size bed, and the living room has a full size sofa bed, with a flat screen TV. There is a private patio right outside the entrance. The marble accented bathroom has a bathtub and shower. A large capacity, in unit washer/dryer is also provided for your convenience."

Let's see how this same description can be transformed to be more compelling. Notice how it comes to life by linking the facts to vivid experiences, as if you were physically walking through the home - room by room.

You'll enjoy walking into this private one bedroom garden flat through it's own separate entrance. With all its amenities, you'll automatically feel right at home.

Living Room
Walk into the expansive living room with a full window wall that looks out to a landscaped patio and view of San Francisco City Hall. It features:
· A pull out sofa bed with full size mattress
· 52" flat screen TV with Comcast's premium package

Kitchen & Dining
The living room opens up into the gourmet kitchen and dining area, where you can enjoy a quiet dinner cooked at home, or delivered from one of our many neighborhood restaurants. Or join the locals and walk to Falletti's one block away. On Sundays, walk to the local Farmer's Market one block away and pick up your favorite fresh produce. The kitchen and dining area feature:
· Dishwasher
· Dining table with seating for 8 people
· Fully equipped kitchen with everything you need to cook meals at home

Bedroom/Bathroom
After a busy day in the city, soak in the bathtub and fall asleep in the quiet and restful bedroom. It offers the best in luxury:
- Tempur-Pedic king size bed
- 100% Egyptian cotton sheets
- Blackout shades
- Carrera marble bathroom
- Quartz countertop
- Glass shower doors
- Luxurious DXV shower head
- Shower and bathtub

Laundry
- Commercial size Maytag washer and dryer
- Steam refresh cycle to refresh your business or cocktail clothes

Do you see how helpful it is to make you feel like you're there? Notice how you can picture yourself using the amenities. This description helps you imagine exactly how the home's location and special features will make your trip a pleasant experience.

Now It's Your Turn….
Write Your Inspiring Listing Description

Worksheet #3

On the following page, I've provided cues to help you easily write an engaging listing description. Answer the questions and use the senses to bring your description to life. When you're finished, you can copy and paste your final version into your listings. You'll find an electronic version of this form in the Library of Templates at https://airbnbtemplates.writerrs.com.

Perfect Host Process™ - Worksheet #3

Write Your Inspiring Listing Description

Instructions: To write your own listing description, answer the questions below. Use the senses to bring your description to life. When you're finished, you can transfer your final version into your listings.

Step 1: Write your introductory sentence using your listing title:
From the moment you arrive at this _____
(i.e. spacious one bedroom apartment) you'll feel right at home.

Step 2: Give the location highlights:
During your stay, you'll especially love that you can:
Ex: walk to Golden Gate Park, see the pier, walk directly to the shuttle service.

Features: **More Living Area Features**
- _____ - _____
- _____ - _____
- _____ - _____
- _____ - _____

Step 2: Take travelers on an imaginary tour of your home:
You'll enter this home through the
Ex: courtyard garden, landscaped patio, desert themed walkway,

_____

_____

Living Area:

Enter the main living area and you'll immediately notice:

Features:

- _____
- _____
- _____
- _____

Describe the experience when you walk in the room.

Ex: you'll love the view of; take an afternoon nap on the couch, relax in front of the fireplace

_____

_____

_____

_____

Kitchen/Dining Area.

You'll enjoy making meals in the kitchen with its *(Ex. Cuisinart Food Processor, gourmet cookware, Vitamix blender, Keurig coffee maker, table in front of the fireplace.)*

- _____
- _____
- _____
- _____
- _____

Bedrooms:

Sink into bed after a day _____

(Ex. touring the city, on the beach). You'll love :

- _____
- _____
- _____
- _____
- _____

Bathrooms:

You'll feel _____

(Ex. relaxed, rejuvenated) from the :

- _____
- _____
- _____
- _____
- _____

Laundry:

You'll enjoy the convenience of _____

(Ex. private laundry, common area laundry) that offers:

- _____
- _____
- _____
- _____
- _____

Outdoor Areas:

Enter the *(private or common area)*_____

(Ex. patio, backyard, roof deck), which is located _____

(right outside your door, across from the property)

_____

Where you'll enjoy:

(Ex. having a family BBQ, reading on the lounge chairs)

- _____
- _____
- _____
- _____
- _____
- _____

Neighborhood Highlights:

Take advantage of *(i.e. LA's finest restaurants, the latest concerts, the area's best surfing)*:

- _____
- _____
- _____
- _____
- _____

Browse my Airbnb Neighborhood Guidebook for local tips!
For insights on local, unique experiences refer your guests to
your neighborhood guide on Airbnb.

Potential Problems:

Are there any potential issues you need to tell your guests

about? If so, list them here, so that your guests will know ahead

of time.

(Ex. Construction noise, parking limitations, anything that may

be out of service)

- _____
- _____
- _____
- _____

Your Persuasive Listing Photos

Travelers will look at photos before anything else when searching through listings. They will literally make or break the decision on booking your home. If you have beautiful photos, you will attract more eyes to your page. Don't assume people will read every detail. Quality photos are the best way to highlight what's special about your space and help travelers book confidently. Here are some tips to make sure your photos are top notch:

- If at all possible, have **professional photos** taken. The bookings you will receive will make it well worth the investment. Airbnb offers free professional photography in some areas. If it's offered in your area, it can take over a month to get a photographer, so be sure to take advantage of it right away!
- **The more photos the better!** Travelers will spend more time on your listing if you have a lot of pictures. Show a variety of shots and scenes giving them a complete idea of what your home is really like.
- Write **detailed captions** for each photo.
- Take pictures **during the day**, turn on all the lights and let as much natural lighting in the rooms as possible. The first hour of sunlight and the last hour of sunlight are considered the best time of day to take pictures outside.
- **Remove all clutter.** It will create a more inviting and welcoming impression. Unnecessary clutter is distracting and prevents people from imagining themselves in your home.

- Add some **welcoming touches** - add some flowers and arrange some magazines on a table.
- Your photos should be a **true reflection of your home** at it's best. Make sure the photos will match what the guests see when they walk in the door. You want your space to look inviting, but don't be misleading.
- **Highlight any special features** you discuss in your description. Include a picture of the barbecue you mention. Highlight a plate of home baked scones and a cup of coffee to show that you offer this in the mornings.
- **Include photos of the outside.** This helps keep guests expectations realistic about what your home looks like on the outside.
- **Include pictures of your neighborhood** to get them excited about their destination. If you're within walking distance of a major attraction, include pictures of that destination. Include pictures of nearby restaurants.

Accurate Descriptions

One of the most common complaints travelers have when giving reviews is when listing descriptions are not accurate. That's why it's critical to explain any potential problems you may be aware of. To do this, you want to provide an accurate description. Make sure you describe anything that may negatively impact their stay. Always remember to manage travelers' expectations with the realities of your home. For example:

"A neighboring historic house is under re-construction and access to the garden area is closed off for now. The apartment unit is very quiet with double-paned, insulated windows, and the bedroom is at the center of the house. That said, there could be noise inside the apartment beyond our control during the usual M-F, 8:00 am - 5:00 pm hours. For this reason, we do not recommend staying with children under 5 who take naps or are light sleepers. If you are an early riser and out visiting the city during the day, this is unlikely to be a problem."

This is one of the easiest ways to ensure you have positive reviews. Travelers do not like surprises! You don't want them imagining your house one way and then experiencing something completely different in person. Providing important details in an organized way saves you time and prevents you from having to respond to complaints and problems later.

Get Feedback From Friends

Sometimes you're so familiar with the details of your home that you inadvertently fail to state an important fact. This causes confusion that you may not be aware of until you get a negative review. That's why it helps to have another person read your listing description before you publish it. Send your description to friends who have been to your home and ask them for their feedback. Was there anything left out that you may have overlooked?

For example, a guest once told me he thought that our roof deck patio was connected to the unit. He was disappointed because that's what he was expecting. It had never occurred to me that guests may have had that impression. I did not say the roof deck was connected to the unit, but I also did not clearly state that it was not. I didn't intentionally mislead him - but that did not matter - he was disappointed. After receiving that guest feedback, I updated my listing to state "You will access the roof deck through a separate entrance that is not directly attached to the unit at the opposite end of the building."

Establish House Rules

Clearly stated House Rules are an important tool in setting expectations for your guests. Airbnb has a specific area for your House Rules when creating your listing. You wouldn't want guests who are planning a party to book your home, if your home is not suitable for parties. You should also include a copy of your House Rules in your physical Guest Welcome Book. We'll discuss this in more detail in the next section of this workbook.

Now It's Your Turn….House Rules Cheat Sheet

On the following page is a House Rules Cheat Sheet that can customize for your own needs. You'll find an electronic version of this form in the Library of Templates https://airbnbtemplates.writerrs.com. You can print this page to place in your Guest Welcome book. Explain what your guests might need to know ahead of time so that they can make their plans with this in mind. For example, if this is not a party house, if you have age limits for booking, etc.

House Rules

Please refer to these House Rules for important information about your stay. If there is anything that requires immediate attention, contact _____ at phone#_____ who will help resolve any issues as quickly as possible. Your alternate local contact is: _____ at phone #_____.

Check-In Time:
Keys/Access Code:
Parking:
WiFi Code:
Property Phone #:

Check-Out Time:
Place keys:
Garbage: Empty garbage into outdoor container
Kitchen: Please wipe down stove, counter tops, sinks and appliances so that they are free of grease and food. Place dirty dishes in dishwasher.

The following items are provided:
Fully equipped kitchen
Bed linens
Extra bed linens located
Towels
Extra towels located
Paper towels, toilet paper, located
Cleaning products including laundry soap, dishwashing liquid, dish soap
Washer/Dryer located
Iron & Ironing board located
Outdoor trash located
Entertainment Items Provided:

Other Household Items:

First Aid Kit, located

Emergency Police/Fire Phone#:

HOUSEKEEPING: Linens and towels are included and are not to be taken from the property. An initial supply of trash liners, toilet paper, paper towels, and soap is provided.

FAMILY RENTAL ONLY: Reservations made for teenagers or young single groups will not be honored without any accompanying adult staying in the property at ALL times. We require at least one member of the party to be at least 25 years of age.

PETS POLICY:

SMOKING POLICY:

Guest agrees to leave the premises and its contents in the same condition, neat and tidy, as guest found the premises to be upon check-in.

The maximum number of sleeping occupants shall not exceed ____ people.

Reservations are not made by or for any person under the age of 25 years old.

Guest and any visitors shall obey all laws of the State of_____, as well as local laws, at all times while they are on the premises. Failure to abide by the laws of _____ or the above rules may cause guest to be asked to vacate the premises and forfeit all rents and security/damage deposits.

Furnishings are not to be removed from the premises for use outside or in other properties.

Guest agrees to provide notice to manager prior to the rental term of any gathering of more than eight (8) people. Property Owner may impose an extra charge at its discretion.

Guest and all other occupants will be required to; 1. Immediately vacate the premises. 2. Forfeit the rental fee and 3. Forfeit the security deposit for any of the following: Overnight occupancy exceeding the _____ person sleeping capacity; total occupancy at any time during the rental term exceeding _____ persons. Using the premises for any illegal activity including the use, possession, or sale of illegal drugs. Causing damage to the premises rented or to any of the neighboring properties. Creating a nuisance by annoying or disturbing other tenants or nearby residents. For example, loud or excessive noise; possessing, using or selling any Fireworks, Firearms, or weapons of any type; jumping from any deck or any place on the property; and any other acts which interfere with the neighbors' right to quiet, quality of life, and enjoyment of their premises.

ENTRY BY OWNER: Property Owner or agent may enter the premises under the following circumstances: in case of an emergency; to make any necessary or agreed upon repairs, alterations, or improvements; supply necessary or agreed upon services or show the premises to prospective purchasers, renters or contractors. Property Owner will provide renter with at least 24 hours notice of Property Owners intent to enter (except in the case of emergency.)

HOLD HARMLESS: The Property Owner and manager, do not assume any liability for loss, damage, or injury to persons or their personal property. Neither does owner accept any liability for any inconveniences, damage, loss or injury arising from any temporary defects or stoppage in supply of water, gas, cable service, electricity or plumbing, as well as due to weather conditions, natural disasters, acts of God, or other reasons beyond its control.

MAINTENANCE: Please report any maintenance needs for the premises to the manager, and we will respond as quickly as possible. Refunds will not be made for maintenance issues including, but not limited to, heating and air conditioning, appliances, televisions, WiFi, and stereos.

LINENS/TOWELS/SUPPLIES: The Property Owners furnish linens and towels. Any lost or damaged linens will be deducted from your deposit. An initial supply of paper products is provided. Extra items needed are the responsibility of the Tenant. Limited cleaning supplies may be provided. We recommend that you bring any special items that you may need.

UTILITIES: No compensation will be given for temporary outage of electricity, gas, water, or cable service, as this is outside of our control. Outages will be reported immediately and all efforts will be made to have them restored as soon as possible. If any utilities are used excessively used (ex. electric bill is 50% higher than previous month) your damage deposit may be impacted.

Maximize Your Profit

As the popularity of Airbnb has increased, more people are jumping on the hosting bandwagon, and this creates more competition. This means your listing must be competitive in every way, including your pricing.

Travel Trends and Pricing

The demand on Airbnb varies by season and tends to correlate with global travel trends. Occasionally, you may notice a drop in the number of bookings and inquiries you receive. When this happens, it pays to do some research. Airbnb hosts in your area may have dropped their prices and are getting all the bookings. Stay informed on the prices of the other listings in your area. Do your own search on Airbnb for similar listings in your area to make sure your prices stay competitive. Here are some other important pricing strategies:

- Airbnb recommends that when you're new to price a little lower until you get some reviews. After you build a few reviews, you can raise your prices in line with your competition.
- Set your rates on a nightly weekly and monthly basis - you may want to provide a discount for longer stays.
- Set Weekend Rates - Demand is higher on the weekends. Compare your rates to your competitors in the area and make sure you are consistent with them.

Create a strategy where you base your pricing on competitive trends, seasons and special events in your area. Some seasonal trends are obvious, such as ski areas in the winter and beach areas in the summer. Other than the seasons, think about what attracts travelers to your area. Is a big game coming to a city near you? Is a major conference coming to your city's convention center? Keep an eye on local event calendars for sporting events, concerts, conferences, etc. If a popular event is coming you may be able to raise your price during those periods. Remember that popular events often book well in advance so it's important to know when they are happening so you can adjust your prices early.

Hotels vs. Airbnb
Be careful when trying to set your rates based on hotel pricing in your area. Airbnb and hotels provide different services. While there will always be a need for the amenities of hotels, the Airbnb experience is different. Travelers may opt for Airbnb over a hotel for usually two reasons: The ability to stay somewhere unique, and the money they can potentially save. If you price yourself like a hotel, you may eliminate as many as half the number of people who may be interested in booking your property.

Is it better to rent your place one third of the time at three times the price, or all the time at one third of the price? The answer is more often at a lower price. People like to save money. So they stay at your reasonably priced Airbnb home, and they leave you a nice review. After a few months, you have a lot of nice reviews. Reviews are what remove the risk of staying at a stranger's house and are the basis to building your Airbnb business.

Be familiar with the hotel rates in your area. This comes in handy when speaking with prospective guests about your pricing. By rationally comparing the value of your home to local hotels, you can highlight the value of your price. For example, a family of four can vacation for a week in a major hotel at $375 per night for 400 square feet with no kitchen. Or they can rent a two bedroom condo with a full kitchen more affordably at $325 a night.

Be careful of leaving your prices too low for too long. If you're finding that you're fully booked for the next 3 months, you might be too low. Keep in mind this rule of thumb:

- At 2-4 weeks out - you should be about 75-90% booked
- At 8-10 weeks out - you should be about 50% booked

You'll notice patterns for your particular area. After several years of hosting, I'm familiar with the pattern for the year. In January and February, I will have fewer inquiries since I'm located in a beach area. My bookings for the winter months are not made as far in advance as they are in the summer months. People visiting my area in winter tend to plan last minute. I know I'll rent during this time, so I set my lower winter rate without any other discounts. As spring approaches, travelers plan their summers. I set my spring rates and summer rates and the summer will become fully booked by the end of May.

Discounts:
In general, only offer discounts if you're uncertain that you'll book the nights. For example, during your off-season it might make sense to offer a special to attract budget conscious travelers. Or, if you have an opening that's only one week away during your peak season, you may fill those nights with lower priced offers at the last minute.

Extra person charges:
How many people does your home sleep comfortably? If you notice guests are often bringing extra people, you may want to charge a fee for each extra person. Make sure you list the maximum occupancy in your rental contract and any extra person charges if they exceed this occupancy.

Finally, don't assume that if you're not getting many bookings that it's because your rates are too high. There maybe other factors involved. Make sure your photos showcase your home and that your listing is well-written and complete. Review your completed Worksheets 1-4 and make sure you followed the steps from the earlier sections of this workbook, and the recommendations from Airbnb.

Avoid confusion between you and your guests. Take advantage of Airbnb's price calculator in your calendar's availability settings allows you to see the price your guests will pay—including taxes, fees, discounts, and more. This helps you understand what travelers actually pay as you establish your prices.

Airbnb Price Tips

It's up to you to determine what you price you want to set for your home. Airbnb aggregates their data based on comparable listings, location and demand and will provide a recommended price. When you set your prices, Airbnb will offer you their price tips directly on your calendar. You my find Airbnb's price tips useful depending on your area. You'll need to decide if it works for you. For example, for this upcoming Memorial Day weekend, Airbnb recommends prices lower than the price I've been getting for the last 3 years on Memorial Day weekend. Perhaps this year will be different due to more competition, so I will consider Airbnb's price tips - but not too far in advance. Also, if you are a new host, you may want to set your prices lower to make sure you're quickly building your bookings and reviews.

Airbnb Smart Pricing

Lets you set your prices to automatically match demand in your area. You enter your minimum price and maximum price.

Airbnb will automatically adjust your price within your parameters based on:

• How many people are searching for listings like yours
• The dates they are searching for
• Whether other listings are getting booked
• Your listing's best qualities

The benefit of Smart Pricing is that it automatically adjusts your price for you. I tried Smart Pricing during the winter months, during my slower season, and I found it did not increase my inquiries or bookings. That said, Smart Pricing may be useful for you, and circumstances may be different in your area.

There are also other pricing tools from available from outside vendors to automate your pricing. They search the web for factors that may impact your rental rates to predict demand on a given day, and then generate pricing recommendations specific to your property. Some of the programs sync with Airbnb to automatically update your listing with the latest prices based on demand. Here are some of the more popular automated pricing tools:

- Everbooked
- BeyondPricing
- PriceLabsCo

Airbnb Fees

Host Fees: It's free to set up your listing on Airbnb - you set your price, security deposit and cleaning fee. Guests pay the full reservation fee to Airbnb at the time of booking. Airbnb collects 3% of what you charge guests as a host service fee. Airbnb holds this money and releases it to you by direct deposit 24 hours after the guest checks in, according to the payout preferences you set up in your Account.

Security Deposits: When you set an amount for the security deposit on your listing, the payment details are stored but the guest is not charged for this amount, unless you make a claim. If you notice damage to your property that you believe to be caused by the guest, you must make a claim within 14 days of when the guest checked out, or before a new guest checks in - whichever is earlier. Airbnb will ask you to provide documentation - such as photos of the damage, along with receipts, invoices, written estimates, or links to comparable items that show the actual cash value for repair or replacement. Airbnb will facilitate the communication through the Resolution Center in your Dashboard and collect payment when necessary.

Guest Fees: Airbnb charges guests 6% - 12% on top of the price you charge. The higher the subtotal before taxes and fees, the lower the Airbnb service fee. It helps to know what guests are ultimately paying when setting your prices because it may impact how they perceive the value of your listing price compared to another.

Occupancy tax - In some cities, Airbnb is now collecting occupancy taxes from travelers and remitting them to the appropriate tax authority. Governments differ on the tax rate, how often it's paid and forms required. For more information, visit the website of your city and county and look up "occupancy tax", "hotel tax", or "transient lodging tax."

Calculate Your Potential Profit

Your Airbnb fees are just some of your expenses associated with your business. To determine your profit, you'll need to account for any other costs associated with your business, such as your mortgage or rent payment, property taxes, insurance, housecleaning services, repairs, and any other related expenses.

You'll receive a Form 1099 (U.S. citizens), or a Form 1042 (non U.S. citizens), that will reflect your total Airbnb revenue for the year to be used for income tax purposes. You can also track your earnings at any time by viewing your Transaction History on the Airbnb website. That's why a separate business account is important - you'll be able to keep track of your business income and expenses more efficiently. An accountant can help you determine which expenses are tax deductible. By organizing your expenses and setting a budget, you can accurately determine your financial goals and create a pricing strategy.

Now It's Your Turn....

Set Your Budget and Pricing

Worksheet #5

Use this worksheet to set your budget and create your pricing strategy. You'll find an electronic version of this form in the Library of Templates at https://airbnbtemplates.writerrs.com. It's important to keep this information updated when you have any changes in costs.

Perfect Host Process™ - Worksheet #5

Pricing for Profit

Use the worksheet on the following page to help you plan your pricing strategy. This will help you determine your income needs and set your budget.

Do Some Research:
Visit Airbnb as a Traveler and do a search for properties in your area that are similar to yours - those with the same number of bedrooms and bathrooms. Find ten properties that are the most similar and look at their prices. Then, look at their calendars to see how booked they are in the future. You'll then make your own assessment of pricing vs. market demand

Add up the nightly rental rate of all ten properties, then divide that total by 10. This will give you an average rental rate for properties like yours in your geographic area. You'll need to make adjustments if some properties have a better location, or are more updated, etc.

Note: Open a separate checking account for your vacation rental business. Keep track of your income and expenses using Quickbooks or other business accounting software. You'll be glad you did when tax time rolls around. Airbnb and FlipKey issue Form 1099's for income tax purposes. HomeAway does not issue 1099's. Some local governments require an occupancy tax, hotel tax or lodge tax to be collected. Check on the requirements for your area. Airbnb automatically collects this tax in certain cities, while HomeAway/VRBO does not and leaves this to you.

Perfect Host Process™ - Worksheet #5

Pricing for Profit

Income:

Average Nightly Rental Rate for Comparable Homes:_____

My Expenses:

Mortgage:_____

Property Taxes:_____

Other Taxes:_____

Utilities:_____

Other Costs:_____

Your Ideal Price:_____

Weekend & Seasonal Demand In Your Area:

When is Your High Demand Season?

_____

Are weekends more popular?

_____

When do major events happen in your area?

_____

_____

_____

_____

_____

Optimize Your Listing

There are some general best practices to ensure your Airbnb listing ranks high on searches. Here are some basic tips to keep in mind:

- Determine the **search terms** that would likely be used by your **ideal guests**. Include these search terms in your listing title and description. Also think of appealing keywords **relevant to your area**, such as landmarks, tourist attractions and local events. When you have targeted search terms that match your listing details, your listing will appear higher in the results.
- Make sure you **have high quality photos**. Professional photos are recommended. In fact, the listing websites will let you know if your photos need improvement. Airbnb will sometimes offer free photography session in select cities, so if it is currently offered in your area, definitely take advantage of this free service. Well photographed listings attract more bookings, so it is worth every penny to have professional photos,
- The more **search permutations** your listing satisfies, the more your property will appear in search results. For example, if you set your minimum stay as one night, it increases the flexibility of your listing - which helps it satisfy more searches, leading to more inquiries and bookings.
- Respond quickly to inquiries. The more **active and responsive** you are the websites, the more favorably you are viewed by the algorithms. This means higher ranking when your property meets a traveler's search criteria, more inquiries, and ultimately more bookings.

- **Log-in and update your calendar** regularly. Hosts who update their calendar at least once a month are approximately 70% more likely to get booked than those who allow their calendar to remain out of date for over one month. I update my calendars at least once a week.
- **Keep your listing fresh.** If your calendar is already up to date, just make a few changes to your calendar. Block a few dates, and then free them up again. This action tends to give a nudge to your listing performance. It signals the algorithm to recognize you.
- **Stay competitive** when setting your listing price. We'll discuss pricing in more detail later in this workbook.
- **Turn on Instant Book.** By turning this feature on, your listing will rank higher - but this means that travelers can book your home immediately without any prior review by you. Remember, host cancellations are negatively viewed by Airbnb, and this can hurt your listing performance, so think carefully before turning on Instant Book. Although you set up your parameters with Instant Book, you must be prepared to commit to all bookings in advance. I prefer to communicate with travelers and find out more about who they are and the purpose of their trip before committing to any booking. I'm not interested in unknowingly hosting a frat on spring break. For that reason, I do not use Instant Book.
- Build your list of **reviews**. A history of reviews (especially positive reviews) will increase your listing's performance as time goes on. We'll discuss creating a review strategy later in this workbook.

- **Avoid cancellations.** Always follow through on your agreements with travelers. Airbnb looks unfavorably on host cancellations and may impose penalties on you, such as a blocked calendar. When you cancel bookings it undermines trust, and this will affect your listing performance.
- A **complete profile** with a solid review history shows you take your business seriously and builds your online trustworthiness as a host. Don't leave any areas blank in your profile.
- Create a helpful **Neighborhood Guidebook** within your listing. Host Guidebooks are often used in recommendation lists that are created by Airbnb. If yours is featured, it will increase your visibility on the site. We'll talk more about how to write a neighborhood Guidebook in the next section.
- **Share your listing** and your host profile on **social media.** Search engines place more trust in something that appears more than once. Promote your "host" persona on your social media accounts - make sure to include links to your Airbnb/HomeAway profiles. You can also share your Airbnb wish lists. All of this activity benefits your search ranking across the internet.
- Take advantage of **Airbnb Wish Lists**. When your listing is saved on someone's Wish List, it helps improve your ranking. Encourage people you know who have Airbnb accounts to save your listing on their Airbnb Wish Lists.

Now It's Your Turn….

Complete the Airbnb SEO Checklist

Turn to your completed Worksheets #2 and #3, the Listing Title Worksheet and Listing Description Worksheet.

Using the **Airbnb SEO Checklist** on the following pages, review your Listing Title and Description. Use the Checklist to make sure you've set your listing up to perform well in possible in searches on Airbnb. You'll find an electronic version of this form in the Library of Templates at https:// airbnbtemplates.writerrs.com.

Airbnb SEO Checklist

1. What search terms would likely be used by your ideal guest? Make sure these terms are included in your description and title.

_____

_____

_____

2. What are appealing keywords relevant to your geographic area? These could be landmarks, tourist attractions and events. Include these terms on your description and title._____

_____

_____

3. Is your profile complete? Do you have every section filled in? _____yes_____no

4. Do you have high quality photos? Do you have enough photos?_____yes_____no

5. Does your listing match as many search permutations as possible? Based on your hosting preferences, how can you match the most searches as possible. For example, a one night minimum stay would match more searches than a four night minimum. Turning on Instant Book makes your listing very flexible. _____yes_____no

6. Are you able to respond to guest inquiries? Have you downloaded your website's apps so that you can respond on the go?_____yes_____no

7. How are you updating your calendar? You should update it at least once a week. Block a few dates, and then unblock them. This will nudge the algorithm to recognize you._____

8. Are your prices competitive? If you're a new host, set your prices lower to start out.

_____yes_____no

9. Are you making sure you build your trust worthiness by avoiding cancellations?

_____yes_____no

10. Are you sharing your listing on your social media accounts?

_____yes_____no

11. Are you building positive reviews? (We'll cover your review strategy in the next section)

_____yes_____no

Action 2: Enhance The Guest Experience

C onsumers today value experiences. Successful companies know this. That's why they focus on creating valuable, customized experiences that consumers cannot get anywhere else. Airbnb knows this too. That's why in addition to offering homes, Airbnb now offers "experience packages" hosted by members of the Airbnb community. Travelers can select experiences from categories such as "Food & Drink", "Art & Design", "Lifestyle", "Sports", "Entertainment", "Nature", "Fashion", "Wellness", "Music" and "History." Understanding your guests and what they want in their getaway helps ensure that they will love staying at your place.

Airbnb has designed the search experience to provide listings that match a traveler's established preferences. So this leads to the question, what will your guest experience be? Travelers on Airbnb have come to expect unique experiences and value, so make sure you are meeting and exceeding their expectations. You can do this through your sense of hospitality, the way you interact with your guests and the value you add to their stay.

Your unique knowledge of your neighborhood is part of what makes you valuable to guests.
Guests appreciate you sharing useful resources in the area such as grocery stores and coffee shops - and tips guests wouldn't expect, like where to find the best pastries or yoga classes.

Your Neighborhood Guidebook

Airbnb provides the option for you to publish a Neighborhood Guidebook with your favorite places to eat and explore in your area. It will appear on your listing page and to your guests. Airbnb also uses your tips along with those of other hosts to create lists of popular places in your geographic area. Your guide could be among those featured in the lists - which could lead to considerable exposure for your listing. Travelers can find everything from coffee shops and parks, to secret spots you recommend. As Airbnb continues to emphasize unique experiences, it will become increasingly common for Airbnb guests to expect this type of hospitality from their hosts. By completing your Guidebook, you are offering your guests a unique perspective that is available only through you.

Now It's Your Turn....

Complete Your Neighborhood Guidebook

Go to your Airbnb Host Dashboard - Find the tab for your Guidebook. Add your tips there. Add your personal tips there. Think of everything you can that would enhance their visit. Remember, guests are looking for a special getaway that is different from staying in a hotel. The little tips are often the most helpful. As an Airbnb Host, you are creating a unique experience for your guest - one that only you can provide.

On your Host Dashboard, simply go to your listing page and select "Guidebook" on the left side of your screen. Select the categories you would like to complete. When you type in a place would like to recommend, it will auto fill the location. You can then add your personal experience and why you are recommending it. Once you have completed your Airbnb Guidebook, you can print it. You'll then add these printed pages to your Guest Welcome Book.

Let's now talk about how to create a Guest Welcome Book.

Your Guest Welcome Book

You're familiar with your home, but your guests aren't. Since you know it well, it can help to learn how it feels to be a guest in your own space. If you haven't stayed in your own space already, stay as a guest there yourself so you can have a sense of empathy for your guests. This can help you learn how to make their experience more positive and comfortable. Your Guest Welcome Book can cover everything from how to access the internet, to finding their way around the kitchen, to anything else that will help them settle in and get comfortable right away. In this section, we'll create your Guest Welcome Book. When it's complete, print it and place all pages in a binder with plastic page protectors. Make sure you place the binder in a central location in plain view so that guests see it when they arrive and can refer to it at any time during their stay.

You'll also want to copy and paste your Guest Welcome Book into your listing for guests to have on the go access to this information. On your Host Dashboard, select the Booking tab on the left of your screen.

Scroll down to "House Rules" and look for the "Additional Rules" box. Click inside this box and paste your entire Guest Welcome Book here. Your guests will then have access to your Welcome Book on the go and prior to their arrival.

Now It's Your Turn….

Create Your Guest Welcome Book

Go to the **Library of Templates** Bonus Material at the back of this book. Locate the **Guest Welcome Book Template** and fill in the blanks to customize it for your needs. You'll then print these pages to place in your binder to display in your property. You'll find an electronic version of this form in the Library of Templates at https://airbnbtemplates.writerrs.com.

Create Your Guest Welcome Book

Instructions:
You'll need the following supplies:

- Binder with a clear plastic sleeve on the cover to insert a cover page.
- Plastic page protectors to keep the pages clean.
- Dividers with tabs. Label the tabs with the following titles:

  1. Welcome Page
  2. Emergency Information
  3. House Rules & Guidelines
  4. Housekeeping & Supplies
  5. Household Equipment
  6. Neighborhood Services
  7. Groceries
  8. Things to Do & Places to Go

- Go to the Guest Welcome Book template in the Library of Templates Bonus Material. Download the Word file at https://airbnbtemplates.writerrs.com. Fill in the blanks on each page to customize it for yourself.
- Print the completed pages and place them under the appropriate tab in your binder.
- Print the pages from your Airbnb Neighborhood Guidebook that you created online in your Airbnb listing. Select the "Print Guidebook" option and place the printed pages in your binder under the tab that is titled "Things to Do & Places to Go."

Your Conversations

By following the Perfect Host Process™ you lay the groundwork for building trust with your guests and a comfortable stay in your home. One of the most important skills of being a successful Airbnb Host is clear communication. From responding to traveler inquiries, answering questions from guests, or corresponding with future guests, you always want to be approachable and welcoming. Understanding their needs helps you make sure that they love staying at your place. Are they looking for peace and quiet? Are they planning a family vacation with kids? Conversations before their stay helps you personalize your hospitality to your guests' needs.

Keep Your Calendar Updated

You may not think of your calendar as a form of communication, but on Airbnb it communicates important information - the dates your home is available for bookings and the dates it is unavailable. More importantly, an updated calendar prevents you from having to cancel any bookings.

To make sure your calendar is current, visit your Host Dashboard and select "Your Listings" then "Calendar." If you list your home on other vacation rental sites, you can choose to synch your calendar with those calendars. To do this, follow the instructions under "Availability Settings." If you know ahead of time that your home will not be available during certain dates, remember to block the dates as "Not Available."

An up-to-date calendar is one of the easiest ways to establish trust with potential guests. You don't want to cancel any reservations or be forced to send an awkward message that your calendar is incorrect. Cancellations are a very bad guest experience. That's why it's important to make sure you do everything possible to prevent cancelling on your guest. For example, Pre-Approve a guest *only* if you are fully prepared to accept the booking. Turn on Instant Book *only* if you are fully prepared to accept all bookings.

Answer Inquiries and Booking Requests Immediately
Your first official conversation happens when you answer an inquiry or booking request from a traveler. Remember to be friendly and approachable in all your conversations, especially this first conversation. **What is an Inquiry?** You receive this message when a traveler is interested in your home and might have some questions. This is your first opportunity to establish rapport. That's why it's important to answer the inquiry immediately. There are several reasons why this is so important. First, it shows warmth and hospitality. Second, the traveler has likely submitted inquiries to more than one host. You don't want to be slow to respond and lose the booking because another host was more responsive. **What is a booking request?** You receive this message when someone has decided to book your home. When you receive a booking request, you can Accept, Decline or send a message if you would like more information.

Set Up Airbnb Notifications

As an Airbnb Host, think of yourself as being "on call." You never know when an inquiry or booking request might come in from across the world. Guests often book with the host that responds first. That's why its important to install the Airbnb app on your phone and set up text and email notifications on your Airbnb account, so that you can respond on the go. You can set this up under "Account Settings" under your profile. Also, make sure the sound is turned up on your phone so that you don't miss a notification. Do whatever it takes to make sure you don't miss notifications on your phone. This is essential to never missing an inquiry or booking. Technically, Airbnb gives you 24 hours to respond to a booking request; however, travelers can change their minds and cancel the request. The slower you are to respond, you increase the chances of losing the booking. On average, most hosts reply to inquiries within 4 hours and accept bookings within 1 hour. So why not be better than average? When following the Perfect Host Process ™ you'll want to reply to inquiries immediately and be ready to accept booking requests within an hour. You'll see how easy this is to do through the use of the **Library of Templates** Bonus Material.

Reviewing the Inquiry or Booking Request

When you receive an inquiry or booking request, double check your calendar to make sure the dates are open. Then read the traveler's message. Most travelers will tell you a little about themselves, who they'll be traveling with and the purpose of the trip. You can usually gain some comfort level through this message. Next, review the traveler's profile. Make sure they have added a photo and notice how the identity was verified. Finally, read through any traveler reviews from other Airbnb hosts. This usually gives me enough information to make a decision. If I still feel like need to learn a little more, I ask for more information. You may need to ask them a few questions to help learn if they would be happy in your space and determine if they are a match. Understanding their travel plans helps you learn what will be important to them.

Accepting or Denying a Booking Request

Once you have made your decision on the booking request, tap the "Accept" or "Decline" button located on the Airbnb Reservation Request message. Should you need to decline the request, you're freeing the traveler to to book another rental. That's why responding within one hour is good customer service.

Choose If You Want To Turn on Instant Book

Instant Book lets you automatically accept reservation requests that fit your pre-set requirements, meaning that you don't need to approve guests before they book - this gives you an excellent response rate in the eyes of Airbnb. But make sure you are prepared to commit to all dates - you don't want to have any cancellations.

Note: Respond to all inquiries and requests! If you let four consecutive reservation requests or booking inquiries expire without responding, Airbnb may temporarily deactivate your listing. They may also deactivate your listing if your response rate is less than 50% across ten bookings.

Keep in mind, if you will be unavailable to host for a certain period of time, you can temporarily pause your listing.

Saving Your Message Templates

You'll also want to include a personal message with your response. You can create Saved Messages for specific purposes to use every time. For example, save a "Thank You for the Reservation" message to send to guests immediately after you accept a reservation. For pre-written messages you can copy and paste into your saved messages, refer to the **Library of Templates** Bonus Material at https:// airbnbtemplates.writerrs.com.

Using saved messages, you can draft and save the answers to your guests' most common questions. For example, you can type directions to your home once, click save, and it will be ready to send to the next guest.

Preparing For Your Guests' Arrival:

It's important to set up a basic arrival routine for each guest:
- Choose a check-in procedure that works for you
- Decide how guests will access your home, whether you'll be there or not
- Create guidelines for key exchange or pick up and drop off

When you provide clear pre-arrival communication and check-in processes, it will help ensure that your guests will have a stress-free arrival.

Here are some important steps to follow before their arrival day:

- Ask for your guests' travel plans so that you can plan convenient check-in times.
- Send them CLEAR instructions on directions to your home and finding the exact location of the property.
- Send them detailed, precise check-in instructions, so they are not left to guess anything. This includes accessing the keys or entry codes.
- Make sure they know how to contact you on arrival day.
- Use email, messaging and texting to be in contact whenever needed.

On the following pages we'll discuss the **Perfect Host Process**™ **Conversation Sequence.** It will provide you step-by-step messaging that will lead to happy guests and a growing collection of Five Star reviews.

Perfect Host Process™ - Conversation Sequence

Message #1
Thank You Message/Email Upon Booking

Message #2
Pre-Arrival Instructions Before Check-In (2 weeks before)

Message #3
After Check-In Welcome

Message #4
How is Everything Going? (Halfway Through Their Stay)

Message#5
Pre-Check-Out Reminder

Message #6
Thank You & Review Request (Immediately After Check-Out)

Download the **Library of Templates** Bonus Material at https://airbnbtemplates.writerrs.com.

There you'll find templates for each of these messages. Copy and paste these messages into your "Saved Messages"in your Airbnb Host Dashboard.

When Your Guest Arrives

When guests arrive, they are usually tired and preoccupied, so you want to make it easy for them to arrive and immediately feel at home. Create a memorable first impression so when they walk in the door they smile and say, "Wow!" The way you welcome guests can set the tone for their entire stay.

Remember, they've planned on a relaxing and fun getaway. They want it to be special, and you don't want to disappoint! What would make you feel at home right away? Empathize with your guests. In fact, if you haven't stayed in your rental home yourself, you need to do this. Look for anything that needs improvement and change anything that would make it more comfortable and functional.

When to Reach Out To Your Guests:

Guests have different preferences for how they interact. Some will contact you often and others will have very little contact unless they need something. Whether you're there or not, they like to know how they can reach you if they have a question or need any help. It's important for you to stay in touch with your guests throughout their stay. That's why Message #3 and Message #4 are so important. Send Message #3 right after they arrive to find out how everything is going and let them know you're available. If they're staying for five days or more, send Message #4 halfway through their stay to check in on them. Just before it's time for them to check out, send Message #5 and ask them if they have any questions. The Perfect Host™ Conversation Sequence is especially helpful with guests who don't say much. They may be unhappy about something and never say a word to you about it. By having a consistent routine you won't have guests feeling like you aren't available or falling through the cracks if they're more quiet.

On the next few pages we'll discuss cleaning and staging your home for your guest's arrival day, as well as welcoming your guest.

Staging Your Home & Greeting Your Guest

Even if you're not there to meet them, you should establish your own greeting routine for your guests. Make sure you're available to answer any questions, especially if you're not there in person. I always plan on responding to messages when I know guests will be arriving. I've learned that following consistent steps for staging my home and greeting every guest the same way every time, ensures things run smoothly. That's why guests are happy when they arrive. This sets the tone for their stay and gets their trip off to a good start.

Making It Extra Special: Ideas That Go Above and Beyond

A thoughtful gesture goes a long way to make them feel welcome. Here are some ideas if you'd like to add a little extra welcome and personality to your home:

Kitchen
- Welcome note
- Coffee with coffee creamer, etc.
- Fruit bowl
- fresh flowers
- Cookies / candy / chocolate on a plate
- Sweets from a local favorite
- bottle of wine & 2 glasses
- recipe book & stand
- bottled water in refrigerator
- useful range of small kitchen appliances
-   such as blender, coffee maker

Laundry
- Basket of special laundry essentials
- Fabric softener
- Laundry soap

Living/Dining Areas
- Bowls with decorative items
- Set dining table with plates, glasses, etc.

Bedroom
- Items for relaxation and comfort
- Picture above bed
- Fresh flowers
- Throw cushions

Bathroom
- Basket of toiletries
- Spa basket

House Cleaning

A clean space is a must - clean spaces make guests feel comfortable from the moment they arrive and can show your commitment to making them feel welcome. After a guest's stay, they can specifically rate the cleanliness of your listing and let future guests know what their experience was like. Cleanliness is the most basic requirement. You don't want negative reviews for cleanliness! Cleaning for guests is different than cleaning for yourself. Guests are expecting to find your place looking like the photos on your listing. Every room should be clean, especially the bathroom and kitchen.

Guest Amenities

Most Airbnb guests expect the following basic amenities:
- High Speed Wireless Internet
- Hairdryer
- Shampoo
- Iron/Ironing Board
- Linens and towels
- Soap
- Toilet Paper

Make sure that each of these items are replenished between each guest, so that they are fresh for the next guest. The **Supplies Checklist** on the following page will help you keep track of supplies you have on hand and those you need to purchase. If your hire a cleaning service provide this checklist to them so that they can inform you when you need to purchase additional supplies. Download this checklist in the **Library of Templates** at https://airbnbtemplates.writerrs.com.

You'll find an electronic version of this form in the Library of Templates at https://airbnbtemplates.writerrs.com.

You'll also find a **Home Staging Checklist** and a **Six Point Cleaning Checklist** to help you prepare for arriving guests.

Proper cleaning takes time and effort. I recommend charging a cleaning fee and paying a housekeeper or service to clean according to these standards. These tasks should be completed for every new guest. The checklists are useful to make sure that everything is done the same way every time - ensuring the best experience for your guests.

Perfect Host Process™ - Supplies Checklist

Household
___Lockable storage shed or cabinets for any personal items you don't want used (clearly marked Owner's Cabinet)
___Fans/Ceiling fans
___Cleaning supplies for guest use
___Windex
___Comet
___Laundry detergent
___Iron/Ironing board
___Paper towels
___Toilet paper
___Light bulbs

Kitchen
___Kitchen supplies for fully functioning kitchen (use the kitchen yourself to make sure)
___Sufficient plates, cutlery and glassware for the maximum people you accommodate
___Sufficient plastic plates, cutlery, glassware for outdoor use
___Wide range of small appliances such as a blender, food processor, waffle maker, slow cooker
___Cooking pans and cooking utensils (in good condition)
___Large pot for boiling corn or cooking pasta.
___Coffee maker

Living/Dining
___Comfortable seating in living area
___Enough seats for the amount of people who stay there

Entertainment/Recreation
___Board games, decks of cards, toys, books clean and in good condition.
___Check board games and cards to ensure they are complete.
___Cooler
___Beach chairs, beach umbrella

Bedrooms
___Mattress covers - replace if needed
___Pillows - replace if stained
___Extra linens, pillows and blankets for each bedroom
___Full length mirror

Bathrooms
___Hair dryer
___Bath Soap
___Hand Soap

Safety/Emergency Supplies
___First Aid Kit
___Functioning smoke alarm
___Functioning carbon monoxide detector
___Functioning fire extinguisher

Posted Emergency Sign*
___Clearly marked fire escape route and map
___Local emergency numbers and the nearest hospital
___Emergency contact number for you and a backup person

*Customize and print the Emergency Sign Template located on the following page. The Word document can be downloaded at https://airbnbtemplates.writerrs.com.

Supply Closet
___Restock paper products (toilet paper, paper towels, coffee filters, etc.).
___Restock cleaning supplies that you leave for your guests including: all purpose leaner/disinfectant, dishwasher detergent, window-cleaner, furniture polish, floor cleaner, and spot remover for carpets.
___Restock trash bags.
___Replace vacuum cleaner bags and provide back-ups.
___Check brooms and mops to see if they need replacing.
___Be sure you have ample supply of back-up supplies that must be replaced more often, such as extra coffee carafe, back-up TV remote controls, extra pillowcases, extra glassware, etc.

in the event of emergency

Fire/Police Emergency Call:

Nearest Hospital:

Host Emergency Phone Number:

Backup Host Emergency Phone Number:

Perfect Host Process™ - Home Staging Checklist

___Curtains open
___A lamp or overhead light on a dimmer
___Ceiling fans on (warm weather)
___No magnets on refrigerator
___Switch on under counter lighting
___Notes placed in strategic places. (i.e., recycling bins labeled,
___how to use the thermostat, how to operate ceiling fans.)
___WiFi code clearly displayed on a note or in a frame
___Guest Welcome Book placed in a prominent location.
___Local brochures of nearby things to do
___Printed neighborhood map
___Designated key area (i.e., on a hook, or basket on kitchen
   counter)
___Keys should be labeled as to what they are used for
___Clean and fresh smelling - no overpowering odors that
   might be unpleasant to some people, or affect allergies
___Fresh towels hanging in the bathroom
___Fresh sheets on the beds
___Folded, nicely presented linens (with no stains or tears)
___Fresh soap in bathrooms and in tubs/showers (Refill liquid
   soap bottles so they are full; replace used bar soap with a
   new bar of soap.)
___Laundry soap in laundry area
___No clutter.
___No dust.
___All dishes are clean and neatly put away. (No dishes in the
   dishwasher.)

Perfect Host Process™ - Home Staging Checklist, cont.

___Clear and clean all countertops

___Small kitchen appliances put in cabinets

___Dish towels clean and folded in drawers; don't leave out

___Cleaning supplies available for guest use

___Closet and/or dresser for guest belongings

___Consider a rack for luggage to create space in the bedrooms

___If you use a lockbox, check to make sure keys are there

___Smoke and carbon monoxide detectors are working; replace batteries if necessary

___Declutter dressers, side tables and coffee tables

___Switch on bedside lamps and side table lamps

___Beds should have attractive, matching linens with plenty of pillows, include extra linens in closets

___Tidy cables in TV areas

___How does the lighting affect the ambience? After dark, does the space feel welcoming and cozy, or dark and unwelcoming? Is there sufficient lighting in living rooms and bedrooms for reading?

___Carpet and rugs free of stains and wear

___Remember to replace anything that looks old or unclean

___Put away personal photos in frames

___Minimal knick knacks

Perfect Host Process™ - Home Staging Checklist, cont.

Exterior:

___Curb appeal
___Entryway and walk-up clear of debris, leaves or fallen branches
___Plants, hanging baskets, planted pots
___Clear of debris
___Do screens need cleaning?
___Does exterior siding need to be power washed?
___Neat and tidy
___Tables/chairs arranged nicely
___Items to be stored are put away neatly
___Clean windows and window sills
___Patio furniture and umbrella - no broken or mildewed pieces
___BBQ with cleaning brush - in working order
___Power wash and paint if needed
___Remove stored materials that could be safety risks for children - fertilizer, rodent poison, flammable liquids

Perfect Host Process™ - Six Point Cleaning Checklist

1. Bathrooms:

___Clean, scrub and sanitize showers, bathtubs, vanity, sinks, and backsplashes.
___Clean mirrors.
___Clean and sanitize toilets.
___Polish chrome.
___Wash floors and tile walls.
___Empty wastebasket.
___Replenish liquid hand soap.
___Clean linens: 2 hand towels, 4 washcloths, 2 bath towels per guest and 1 shower mat.

2. Bedrooms:

___Change sheets/pillowcases (no stains or tears)
___Mattress clean and free of mildew and damp smells
___Check for evidence of bed bug activity
___Mattress cover in good condition - replace stained or worn
___Clear area to create space for unpacking
___Dust furniture and clean mirrors.
___Vacuum floor and under beds
___Check for personal belongings left in drawers and closets.
___Check windows for fingerprints.
___Make sure light bulbs are not burned out.
___Check for wear and tear/stains on pillows, sheets, blankets.
___Wash blankets and comforters after every 10 rentals.

Perfect Host Process™ - Six Point Cleaning Checklist

3. Kitchen
___Clean refrigerator inside & out: remove old food
___Clean appliances, counters, cabinets, table, and chairs.
___Clean, scrub, and sanitize sinks, countertops, and backsplashes.
___Clean range top and wipe out inside of oven.
___Clean appliance exteriors, including the inside of toaster and coffee maker.
___Clean inside and outside of refrigerator and microwave oven. Wash/mop floor.
___Empty dishwasher, and quickly organize cupboards.
___Restock auto dish detergent, liquid dish soap, coffee filters, and trash bags.
___Put out 2 clean dishtowels,and a new sponge.

4. Living Room
___Clean, dust, and vacuum.
___Dust window sills and ledges.
___Dust furniture, blinds, picture frames, knickknacks, ceiling fans, and lamps.
___Vacuum carpets or wash floor.
___Vacuum furniture, including under seat cushions.
___Check sofa bed for dirty linens.
___Wash windows on sliding glass doors.
___Empty and clean wastebaskets.
___Be sure to leave clean linens for the sofa bed.

Perfect Host Process™ - Six Point Cleaning Checklist

5. Other areas
___Be sure washer and dryer are empty; clean out lint trap.
___Check light bulbs, change if necessary.
___Once per month, change furnace filter.
___Wipe off patio set, clean barbeque grill.
___Notify owner immediately if you notice any damages, missing items, or if the home was left excessively dirty.

6. Monthly Tasks:
Date Last Performed_____

___Spot clean walls, doorknobs, light switches
___Extra dusting of wall art, mirror frames, ceiling fans, etc.
___Clean baseboards
___Steam clean carpets
___Check for signs of bugs or pests
___Replace batteries in smoke detectors and carbon monoxide detectors
___Check pressure gauge on fire extinguisher
___Replace furnace and air filters
___Vacuum vents and behind large furniture
___Vacuum lint trap on the dryer and wash inside of washing machine
___Clean windows
___Wash curtains or clean window blinds
___Guest Welcome Book should be clean and free of stains, creased or torn pages, etc. - replace with fresh pages or a new binder if necessary

Perfect Host Process™ - Six Point Cleaning Checklist

List of any missing/damaged items from this changeover

Date _____

Include details of damaged or missing items.

_____
_____
_____
_____
_____
_____
_____
_____
_____
_____
_____

Other Notes:

_____
_____
_____
_____
_____
_____
_____
_____
_____
_____

Handling The Unexpected

If you've hosted on Airbnb long enough, chances are at one time or another the unexpected will happen. Whether it's a plumbing problem, a lost garage door opener, or disruptive noise from construction, the question is not *if* things will go wrong, it's *when* they will go wrong. The most important part of handling a problem is to be responsive. Always make sure you can be reached. Be available to communicate as needs come up. If you're not there or cannot be available, make sure to provide an alternate contact person in case something comes up.

Apologize Quickly…Among hundreds of guests, things are bound to go wrong at times.

I once had a guest who was disturbed by noise from upstairs that was beyond my control. When she complained to me I quickly apologized. This is the text message I received early one morning:

"It's after 2 am and the people upstairs have been loud for hours. I suffer from insomnia and can't get any rest on a much needed vacation!"

My reply:

"I am so sorry. I have contacted the person upstairs and have asked him to lower his volume. I would like to make this up to you in some way. I'll be in touch later this morning."

I had not yet determined how to compensate this guest, but I made sure to reply to her message right away, so that she knew I was taking steps to improve the situation.

...Then Go the Extra Mile

Later that morning I sent her this message:

"I would like treat you $50 to Happy Hour. Let me know when and where you would like to go, and I will call ahead. I recommend the rooftop bar at Hotel Erwin. It's a popular spot, so I would recommend reservations."

Her reply:

"Thank you so much! We have a 6:30 reservation at the bar at the Hotel Erwin."

What could have become a terrible review, became a 5 Star Review that has lead to many more bookings.

Always Follow Up - Check back in with your guests after you have worked to resolve the problem and ask them if the situation has improved. This lets guests know that you sincerely care about their experience.

Ideas for Going the Extra Mile:
- Happy Hour drinks at a favorite local restaurant
- Amazon gift card
- Airbnb credit

Guest Checkout

Pre-Checkout Reminder

Just as with welcoming your guest, setting up a consistent routine when your guest leaves makes things run smoothly. Leave a printed **Guest Checkout Checklist** next to your Guest Welcome Book, so they have an easy way to refer to the check-out steps.

The day before they check-out, send your guests a pre-checkout reminder message. This gives you a chance to remind them of your check-out procedures and ask them to tell you about any areas of improvement they noticed. They can either write their feedback on the **Guest Checkout Checklist,** or reply directly to your message. This lets them know that you genuinely want their feedback. If they have any concerns or negative feelings, it gives them a chance to let you know privately - before posting anything on a public review. It gives you a chance to address those concerns, making it more likely that they will then leave you a positive review.

Now It's Your Turn....

**Send Message #5 Pre-Checkout Reminder
(1 day before checkout)**

Create Your Guest Checkout Checklist

In the **Library of Templates** Bonus Material at https://airbnbtemplates.writerrs.com, you'll find a fillable form you can customize to create your Guest Checkout Checklist. Print a copy and leave it next to your Guest Welcome Book, so that guests can locate it easily. Even though you may have this listed in other places, many guests will still ask what your checkout procedures are. Having a printed copy for them saves them the effort of asking you what they should do before they leave.

To send your Pre-checkout Reminder use the template for **Message #5**, located in the **Library of Templates** Bonus Material at https://airbnbtemplates.writerrs.com. You should have also saved this message to your Airbnb saved messages.

Guest Checkout Checklist

Thank you for staying with us! We hope you had a wonderful time! Before you leave, it would be helpful if you do the following:

Keys:

Sheets/Towels:

Kitchen:
___Counter tops should be clear and wiped down.
___Place any dirty dishes in dishwasher and started.
___Empty refrigerator of any perishable food.

Garbage:
Please empty the garbage and take to the cans located_____
Recycling is placed_____

AC/Heating Thermostats:

Other Instructions:

Outdoor Instructions:

___Please double check that you have all your personal belongings, especially phone chargers.

Guest Checkout Checklist

Your feedback is important!

If you had anything go wrong or have suggestions for ways we could improve, could you please write your comments below and let us know?

_____

_____

_____

_____

_____

_____

Predictable Positive Reviews

One of the essential elements of the Perfect Host Process™ is that you're initiating the conversation, not responding. You're a proactive host, not a reactive host. The grand finale of this process is the Guest Review - it's a key part of building a successful Airbnb business. Your business and the Airbnb community rely on these reviews, and guests rely on reviews when they decide where to book. If you've followed **Perfect Host Process™ Conversation Sequence** we discussed in the previous section, positive reviews will become a predictable result, every time!

When I first started hosting, there would be times when something had gone wrong for a guest, and I was not aware of it. Because they never mentioned it to me, I assumed everything was fine. Then I was blindsided by a negative review. This happened to me more than once, and it's why I created the **Perfect Host™ Conversation Sequence** we've been discussing. By following this formula, you will have very few surprises, if any. Without this level of ongoing communication, you won't always know if guests were unhappy - until they leave you a negative review. You can't rely solely on Airbnb's automated messaging to do this for you.

Now It's Your Turn....

Send Message #6 Thank You & Review Request (Immediately After Check-Out)

Download the template for Message #6, located in the **Library of Templates** Bonus Material at https://airbnbtemplates.writerrs.com. Remember to also keep this in your Airbnb saved messages. It's a simple message that is sent immediately after check-out:

"Thank you for staying with me. I hope you enjoyed your time in Los Angeles. I work very hard to make sure all of my guests have a wonderful stay. This property is my small family business, and a 5-Star Review goes a long way for us! If you enjoyed your stay and wouldn't mind, could you please write a review about your favorite parts of our home? I would really appreciate it!"

Then, pay close attention the feedback you receive from these messages and from your reviews. It's valuable information you can use it to improve and update your listing. You might find out you need to upgrade your amenities, or update your listing to be more accurate.

Leaving Your Guest a Review

At the same time you send the Thank You message, leave your guests a review. This is another chance to thank them and provide helpful feedback. When you are the first to leave a review, it encourages guests to leave a review for you.

Cleaning and Changeover

Once they have left, use the **Six Point Cleaning Checklist** and **Supplies Checklist** to make sure everything is in order. Make sure to give a copy to your house cleaning service or any other people who help you with guest changeovers.

During the changeover, anything missing or damaged should be documented by you, your house cleaner, or another person you designate. On the last page of the Six Point Cleaning Checklist, you'll find an area to document this information. Keep in mind that Airbnb requires proof of value when making a claim - which would include photos and/or video along with receipts, invoices, written estimates, or links to comparable items denoting actual cash value for repair or replacement.

If you often have back-to-back guests leaving and arriving on the same day, you will need to be strict with your check-in and check-out times. You will avoid a lot of problems if you clearly state your policy in your check-in and check-out instructions. Make sure you allow plenty of time to clean the property and change the laundry. You also need to allow time to deal with any issues that might be discovered during the changeover.

While guests appreciate flexibility in arrival and departure times, you must specify that they ask ahead of time for any changes to the schedule. If I have a day or more free between bookings, and a guest has a later flight or arrives early, I'm more than happy to accommodate late departures and early arrivals at no additional cost. Guests have told me they really appreciate this flexibility which has led to very positive reviews.

Action 3: Assemble Your Tools

Your Schedule

I f you have multiple properties, or are managing remotely, it's difficult to be in multiple places at once. That's when automation tools make the difference.

Self Check-In Tools
Airbnb has an option where you can choose "Self Check-In" on your listing - this is highlighted on your listing, which some travelers like. There are a few options available for automating check-in:

1. Electronic Locks
Electronic code locks replace your deadbolt and allow entry via a punch-in code. It also allows you to generate a new code for each guest.

2. Lockbox with Key
This choice is somewhat less secure since you cannot change keys after every guest. Simple combination key boxes are an inexpensive option for ensuring your guests get their keys no matter what time of day they arrive.

3. Smart Locks
These devices use an electronic system which allow property access when it receives a wireless signal (often via Bluetooth) from a verified smartphone. That means you can remotely grant access to a guest a few hours before check-in to keep things really simple.

4. Co-Manager, or Concierge Service

If you prefer to keep the personal touch of greeting upon arrival, you can hire someone else take care of it for you. Vacation rental concierge companies can also provide welcome tours of your home, carry out security checks and even attend to laundry and housekeeping between guests. Airbnb has the option for you to designate a Co-Host - who would have access to your Airbnb Host Dashboard and messaging.

Airbnb Calendar Settings

Your Airbnb calendar settings have some options that can help you manage your bookings efficiently. For example, some hosts prefer to block time between bookings to prepare for their next guests or manage time for cleaning. To do this you can automatically block a day or two between bookings.

You can also avoid same-day or next-day requests by selecting the appropriate option on your calendar settings.

The calendar settings allow you to control how far in advance you want to schedule bookings. For example, you can prevent reservation requests that are more than three months in the future, or allow bookings more than a year in advance.

The "preparation time" feature lets you automatically reserve up to two days between bookings. You can also adjust check-in and check-out times to leave yourself more time, as well as think ahead and block longer periods of time when you need a break from hosting.

Email Management:

When you receive a message, text or email, it's helpful to ask yourself these questions:

1. Is this from a current guest? If so, it needs to be answered immediately. For all other messages…

2. Can this request be done in two minutes or less? If the answer is yes, do it immediately.

3. Can it be handled by someone else? If the answer is yes, forward the request to that person.

4. Can this wait? Maybe it is a request that will take longer than two minutes, and you can't delegate it to someone else. So you consciously decide to defer it. Add it to your To-Do List and schedule time on your calendar to complete it.

What if the message is not asking you to do anything? Maybe someone is just providing you information. In that case, you need to decide if it's information you might need later. If so, then file it. When in doubt, file it. You can always delete it later. Keep your files simple. I prefer to use one folder labeled "archived". Too many folders gets complicated. Before you know it you can't find something, you've forgotten where or why you filed it in a certain folder. This leads to procrastination.

Email Management Tools:

Take advantage of the filter rules available to you in your email program. You can create your own rules such as emails from certain senders, or certain types of emails can be automatically sent to their own folder. For example, once a month, your homeowners association sends you the minutes from the last board meeting. You can set up these emails to automatically go into a "Homeowner's Association" folder. They can stayed queued for you there, still unread. This allows you to prioritize your emails.

There are some email management tools available that are easier to use than email filters. Here are a few:

- **SaneBox** will sort your inbox for you before you even look at it. It can move all the emails you subscribe to, such as newsletters to a special folder you designate. That means the only things you see in your inbox are the important emails that you want, such as personal or professional messages from real people. All the promotions, newsletters, receipts can be sorted for you before you even check your email.
- **UnrollMe** consolidates unsubscribing for you. It segregates out every email that has an "Unsubscribe" link and provides you a list in one email where you can decide whether or not to unsubscribe to each one individually, or just unsubscribe to the entire list. You can elect how often UnrollMe sends you this list.

Identify common requests and create templates for the answers.

You'll notice a pattern in questions that guests will often ask you. When you notice these common questions make sure the information is clearly written in your Guest House Manual or Welcome Book - if you're getting repeated questions on something there is a good chance you have not provided clear instructions, or the information is hard to find. To save time, let pre-written responses answer the questions for you. So when you get one of these common questions or requests, pull up the template, such as "Bike Lock Combinations" You can modify the language to personalize it, and hit send. If I'm responding by email, I have my common responses saved as different email signatures.

If I'm text messaging, I create pre-written text messages and save them in my "Notes" app, and then copy and paste the message I need in the new text.

Your People

Assemble Your Local Team
- Handyman, housekeeper, plumber
- Internet Provider phone number, account number
- TV Cable company phone number, account number
- Local point of contact for guests if you're not close by - friend, neighbor, Airbnb co-host, professional concierge service

Now It's Your Turn....

Your Local Team List Cheat Sheet

Refer to the following **Local Team List Cheat Sheet**. You'll also find this template at https://airbnbtemplates.writerrs.com in the Library of Templates. Download the file and customize this list for your own needs. Fill it with your necessary information to keep as a quick reference.

Perfect Host Process ™

My Local Team List

House Cleaning

Services:_____

Handyman:_____

Plumber:_____

Internet Service

Provider:_____

Account

Number:_____

Security Information required when

calling :_____

TV Service

Provider:_____

Account

Number:_____

Security Information required when calling

in:_____

Backup Point of Contact Person

(Local):_____

LIBRARY
OF
TEMPLATES

To download electronic documents, visit

https://airbnbtemplates.writerrs.com

Perfect Host Process™ Conversation Sequence

Messaging Templates

The **Perfect Host Process™ Conversation Sequence** is step-by-step messaging that will lead to happy guests and a growing collection of Five Star reviews. Copy and paste these messages into your "Saved Messages"in your Airbnb Host Dashboard.

Message #1 - Thank You Message/Email
(Upon Booking)

Message #2 - Pre-Arrival Instructions Before Check-In
(2 weeks before)

Message #3 - After Check-In Welcome

Message #4 - How is Everything Going?
(Halfway Through Their Stay)

Message#5 - Pre-Check-Out Reminder

Message #6 - Thank You & Review Request
(Immediately After Check-Out)

Perfect Host Process™ Conversation Sequence

Message #1
Thank You For The Reservation
(Upon Booking)

This message is sent immediately after you accept the reservation request.

Hi Guest Name,

Thank you for for the reservation request. I have confirmed your reservation for the dates you requested. We look forward to having you stay with us in City Name!

I'll be in touch as we get closer to your arrival date with your welcome information.

Happy Travels!
Your Name
cell phone number
email address

Perfect Host Process™ Conversation Sequence

Message #2
Pre-Arrival Instructions
(2 weeks before check-in)

This message is sent 2 weeks before the guest's arrival date. Attach your own check-in instructions as a separate PDF file.

Hi Guest Name,

We look forward to having you stay with us in City Name! We have you booked for the following times:

Check-In: date, at time
Check-Out: date, at time

We often have other guests leaving and arriving on the same day, so we would very much appreciate it if you would be considerate of this schedule.

Attached you will find your Welcome Instructions that include the address and important information on how to access the keys, directions on locating the property and more.

I'm here to help, so please feel free to contact me by phone, email or text message should you have any questions.

Your Name
cell phone number
email address

Perfect Host Process™ Conversation Sequence

Message #3
Check-In Welcome
(immediately after arrival)

This message is sent immediately after the guest's arrival.

Hi Guest Name,

Welcome to City Name! I hope you were able to find my home and that you're getting settled in and comfortable there. Please check everything for cleanliness and let me know if anything needs attention, and I'll make sure it's taken care of for you.

Make sure you look over the Guest Welcome Book in the binder. It contains household information which you may find helpful. It also contains my personal tips and recommendations for restaurants and places to go in the area.

I'm here to help, so please feel free to contact me by phone, email or text message should you have any questions.

Enjoy Your Stay!

Your Name
cell phone number
email address

Perfect Host Process™ Conversation Sequence

Message #4
How Is Everything?
(halfway through their stay)

This message is to touch base with your guest to make sure everything is going well. It should be sent halfway through their stay.

Hi Guest Name,

Just touching base with you. I hope you're enjoying your stay in City Name and that everything has been going well. I'm here to help so please let me know if you need anything or if you have any questions at all.

Cheers!
Your Name
cell phone number
email address

Perfect Host Process™ Conversation Sequence

Message #5
Pre-Checkout Reminder
(1 day before check-out)

This message is to remind your guests of their check out time and procedures. It also gives them a chance to express any concerns now before posting any reviews. It should be sent the day before their departure.

Hi Guest Name,

Look over the Guest Checkout Checklist that was placed next to the Guest Welcome Book. It has some friendly reminders of just a few things to take care of before leaving the home.

You'll also see some space for comments. I work very hard to make sure all of my guests have a wonderful stay. So, if you had anything go wrong or have suggestions for ways I could improve, could you please include them? Or you can reply to this message and let me know.

I welcome this feedback and want to know if there is anything I need to change for the future.

Thank you for staying with us! We hope you had a wonderful time!

Cheers!
Your Name
cell phone number
email address

Perfect Host Process™ Conversation Sequence

Message #6
Thank You and Review Request
(immediately after check-out)

This message should be sent immediately after your guests leave. It is a simple way to encourage them to leave you a positive review.

Hi Guest Name,

Thank you for staying with me. I hope you enjoyed your time in City Name. I work very hard to make sure all of my guests have a wonderful stay. This property is my small family business, and a 5-Star Review goes a long way for us! If you enjoyed your stay and wouldn't mind, could you please write a review about your favorite parts of our home? I would really appreciate it!

We enjoyed having you!

Your Name

cell phone number
email address

Guest Welcome Book

Welcome!

Welcome to my home. I'm glad you're here, and I want to make sure you have everything you need to feel comfortable at home. This Welcome Book will help you with important information about your stay. If there is anything that requires immediate attention, please let me know, and I will help resolve any issues as quickly as possible.

Property Address:

Property Telephone:

Host Name:

Host Phone Number:

Host Email Address:

Check-In Time:

Check-Out Time:

Check-Out Instructions:

Please Note: I may or may not be present at the time of your departure, but I will perform a walk through that same day to make sure everything is in order so that your security deposit can be returned to you as soon as possible.

WiFi name:

WiFi Password:

Key Location/Access Information:

Parking Information:
Emergency Information:

Police/Fire:

Emergency Hospital:

Urgent Care:

Local Natural Disaster Instructions:

House Rules & Guidelines

My home is your home during your stay, and the building and surrounding area is the community you share with the other residents. These rules and guidelines are not intended to be restrictive but are designed to help create a better, more pleasant and safer place for everyone. A friendly cooperative spirit will be to the benefit of all. I solicit your help in attaining these goals.

Quiet Hours: This is a residential community, and your residential unit is not a "party house." As with any residential community, there are city noise ordinances; therefore, please be respectful and considerate of the home, the property and the neighbors in the community. Please pay special attention to the following rules and guidelines related to noise levels:

- All musical instruments, television sets, radios, stereos, etc. are to be played at a low volume during "quiet hours," 10 p.m. to 8 a.m., and at any other time are to be played only at a moderate volume so as not to disturb other residents or neighbors.
- No unnecessary noise or loud talking, and no amplification of any kind (except for inside music or TV), is allowed at any time (no exceptions).
- Drunkenness/intoxication, disorderly conduct, objectionable language or other disturbance is not allowed. Please be aware of speaking volume when alcohol is being consumed, as volume tends to be higher under these conditions.
- Disorderly conduct includes running or talking loudly, yelling or screaming, or otherwise harassing people on the sidewalk or alley below. A "party" fee of between $100-$500 will be imposed, to cover the cost of supervision to assure that violation of city noise ordinances does not occur and that other guests, residents or neighbors are not disturbed. An additional security deposit may be required in order to continue the tenancy. If there is more than one occurrence, additional fee(s) will be incurred.

Common Areas:

The following areas are available only to you and your guests:

During these hours:

Please respect these times. Any complaints from a resident or neighbors could lead to loss of your security deposit and/or possible eviction.

After you are finished using these areas, please pick up ALL TRASH and take it with you to the trash cans. Please remember to respect our neighbors on all sides of the building.

Pet Policy:

No Smoking: in the rental unit or anywhere on or near the property. In addition, smokers may not smoke near enough to the property such that smoke could blow/flow onto any area of the property. Cigarette butts shall be completely extinguished and disposed of in public trash cans, and shall not be thrown on the premises or the street. If it is determined that someone has smoked in the rental unit or anywhere on or near the property, or near enough to the property to cause smoke to blow/flow onto the property, or has put their cigarette butts anywhere other than the public trash cans, there will be a minimum $250 fee per occurrence, in which case an additional security deposit may be required in order to continue the tenancy. If there is more than one occurrence, additional fee(s) will be incurred.

Housekeeping & Supplies

Extra linens and pillows are located:

Washer/Dryer is located:

Iron & ironing board is stored:

Hair dryer is stored:

Cleaning supplies are stored:

Other Supplies:

Outside Trash Is Located:

Trash Pick Up Day Is:

Groceries

Below are are my recommendations for grocery shopping in the area:

Grocery Stores:

Grocery Delivery:

Pharmacies

Household Equipment

Furniture: Please do not move the furniture. You will be charged for repair of any scratches to the floor caused by moving the furniture. If you desire to move any furniture, please call your host for assistance as it must be lifted/carried by more than one person and not pushed or dragged.

Household Malfunctions: Please immediately report to the manager any breakage or malfunction of the appliances, plumbing, television, etc. to make sure the property can be maintained properly.

Operating Instructions for Household Equipment (TV Remote, Coffee Maker, etc.):

Neighborhood Services:

Below are are my recommendations in the event you have a need for the following services:

Auto Repair:

Dry Cleaning:

Pet Boarding:

Beauty:

Florist:

Final Notes

Thank you for purchasing this workbook. I sincerely hope it organizes your life as an Airbnb Host and helps you accomplish more in less time. Feel free to tweak my recommendations for your own needs, depending on your home and location. The best part about having an organized system is that once you get it up and running, it's like a well-oiled machine that gives you predictable, positive results and helps you take control of your time.

Remember to download the Library of Templates Bonus material at https://airbnbtemplates.writerrs.com. You'll also find some extra gifts there too!

I wish you much success ahead!

About The Author

In addition to her experience as a successful Airbnb host, Sandra Shillington is a copywriter and instructional designer. She helps businesses craft the perfect message. Sandra is Founder and Head Writer and founder at Writerrs.com, providing flat rate copywriting services to businesses. She has a BS is Business Administration from Pepperdine University.

Made in the USA
Middletown, DE
23 November 2019

79314333R00071